· *Cooking for Today* ·

CHILDREN'S PARTY CAKES

·*Cooking for Today*·

CHILDREN'S PARTY CAKES

ROSEMARY WADEY

SIENA

A Siena Book
Siena is an imprint of Parragon Books

First published in Great Britain in 1996 by
Parragon Book Service Ltd
Unit 13–17
Avonbridge Trading Estate
Atlantic Road
Avonmouth
Bristol BS11 9QD

ISBN 0-7525-1469-5

Produced by Haldane Mason, London

Printed in Italy

Acknowledgements:
Art Direction: Ron Samuels
Editor: Joanna Swinnerton
Series Design: Pedro & Frances Prá-Lopez/Kingfisher Design
Page Design: Somewhere Creative
Photography: Joff Lee
Styling: John Lee Studios
Home Economist: Rosemary Wadey

Photographs on pages 6, 18, 30, 48 and 66 reproduced by permission of
ZEFA Picture Library (UK) Ltd.

Note:
Cup measurements in this book are for American cups. Tablespoons are assumed to be 15 ml.
Unless otherwise stated, milk is assumed to be full-fat and eggs are AA large.

Contents

✤

CHAPTER ONE

Basic Recipes

❦

A child's party cake is a wonderful invention; sometimes long-awaited, sometimes a complete surprise, but always delicious and thrilling for an already excited child.

When you have decided what the theme of cake is going to be, the next important things to decide are the type and flavour of the cake, the filling, icing (frosting), colour and decoration, and whether it should have any extra decorations, such as candles. The type of cake must suit the design you have chosen. For instance, if it is to be cut and shaped, the cake should be fairly firm, and here a Madeira (Pound) Cake is best, as it keeps its shape and moistness and is easy to coat in either butter cream or sugarpaste. For marzipan-lovers, a layer can be added beneath any type of icing (frosting), or it can be used to mould figures and decorations in the same way as sugarpaste. Quick Mix Cakes can be used widely too, but the Victoria Sandwich (Sponge Layer Cake) has a much softer texture and is best for a cake without too much sculpture involved.

Whatever cake you choose, you should leave it to rest on a wire rack with the lining paper attached for at least twelve, and preferably twenty-four, hours before you begin to cut or decorate it. When it has been allowed to 'set' in this way, it will firm up slightly, and cutting, icing and decorating it will be a lot easier.

Opposite: *Every cake is as good as its basic ingredients, so choose the best quality you can to be sure of a delicious result.*

STEP 3

STEP 4

STEP 5

STEP 6

VICTORIA SANDWICH (SPONGE LAYER CAKE) & QUICK MIX CAKE

The favourite sponge cake and its very quick alternative, both of which, either plain or flavoured, are ideal for these children's cakes. See page 77 for the quantities needed for different sizes of cake.

MAKES A 30 × 25 CM/12 × 10 INCH CAKE

350 g/12 oz/1½ cups butter or margarine for Victoria Sandwich (Sponge Layer Cake) or 350 g/12 oz/1½ cups soft margarine for Quick Mix Cake
350 g/12 oz/1½ cups caster (superfine) sugar; or light soft brown; or half each caster (superfine) and soft brown
6 eggs
350 g/12 oz/3 cups self-raising flour, sifted
2 tbsp water for Victoria Sandwich (Sponge Layer Cake) only
few drops of vanilla flavouring (extract)
3 tsp baking powder for Quick Mix Cake only
apricot jam, sieved (strained)
butter cream (see page 15) to decorate

1 For either cake, grease and line a rectangular cake or roasting tin (pan) about 30 × 25 cm/12 × 10 inches with baking parchment.

2 For the Victoria Sandwich (Sponge Layer Cake), cream the butter and sugar together until light, fluffy and pale. Beat in the eggs, one at a time, following each with a tablespoonful of the flour. Fold in the remaining flour, then the water and vanilla flavouring (extract).

3 To make the Quick Mix Cake, put the fat, sugar, eggs, flour, vanilla flavouring (extract) and baking powder into a bowl and beat vigorously for 2 minutes either by hand, using a hand-held electric mixer, or in a large free-standing mixer.

4 Spread either cake mixture evenly into the prepared tin (pan), level the top and make sure there is plenty of mixture in the corners. Bake in a preheated oven at 180°C/350°F/Gas Mark 4 for about 50–60 minutes for the Victoria Sandwich (Sponge Layer Cake), or about 1–1¼ hours for the Quick Mix Cake, until well risen and firm to the touch. Invert carefully on a wire rack and leave to cool. If possible leave for 12–24 hours to 'set' (see page 7).

5 Use this size of cake for the following numeral cakes: 2, 5, 6, 7 and 9. Make a template (see page 78) and place on the cake.

6 Cut carefully around the template with a serrated knife. Transfer the cake to a suitable-sized cake board, brush with sieved (strained) jam (see page 12) and decorate with butter cream.

STEP 4

STEP 5

STEP 6

STEP 7

MADEIRA (POUND) CAKE

This is probably the best cake to use for novelty cakes, as it has a slightly firmer texture, which makes it easier to shape. See page 77 for the quantities needed for different sizes of cake.

MAKES A **23 CM/9 INCH DEEP ROUND OR SQUARE CAKE OR 25 CM/10 INCH SHALLOW ROUND OR SQUARE CAKE**

300 g/10 oz/1¼ cups butter or margarine
300 g/10 oz/1¼ cups caster (superfine) sugar
5 eggs
300 g/10 oz/2½ cups self-raising flour
150 g/5 oz/1¼ cups plain (all-purpose) flour
grated rind of 2 large lemons
2 tbsp lemon juice

1 Grease and line a 23 cm/9 inch round or square cake tin (pan); or a 25 cm/10 inch round or square cake tin (pan) with baking parchment.

2 Cream the butter or margarine and caster (superfine) sugar together until very light, fluffy and pale in colour, then beat in the eggs, one at a time, following each with a tablespoonful of the flour.

3 Sift the remaining flours together and fold them into the creamed mixture, followed by the grated lemon rind and juice. Spoon the mixture into the prepared tin (pan) and level the top, making sure there is plenty of mixture in the corners.

4 Bake in a preheated oven at 160°C/325°F/Gas Mark 3 for about 1¼–1½ hours for the 25 cm/10 inch tin (pan); or about 1½–1¾ hours for the 23 cm/9 inch tin (pan), until the cake is well risen, golden brown and firm to the touch. Cool in the tin (pan) for a few minutes, then invert on a wire rack to cool. Leave to set (see page 7).

5 Use a 23–25 cm/9–10 inch square cake for a 0 or 4 numeral cake. Draw a template and cut it out (see page 78). Position the template on the cake and cut carefully around it, using a serrated knife.

6 Use 2 × 20 cm/8 inch round cakes (using the 4-egg mixture: see page 77) for a 3 or 8 numeral cake. The template for the number 3 cake can be made by drawing a figure of 8, then cutting out a section of the card to make the 8 into a 3, as shown.

7 Decorate the cake on the cake board with butter cream, sugarpaste and/or royal icing.

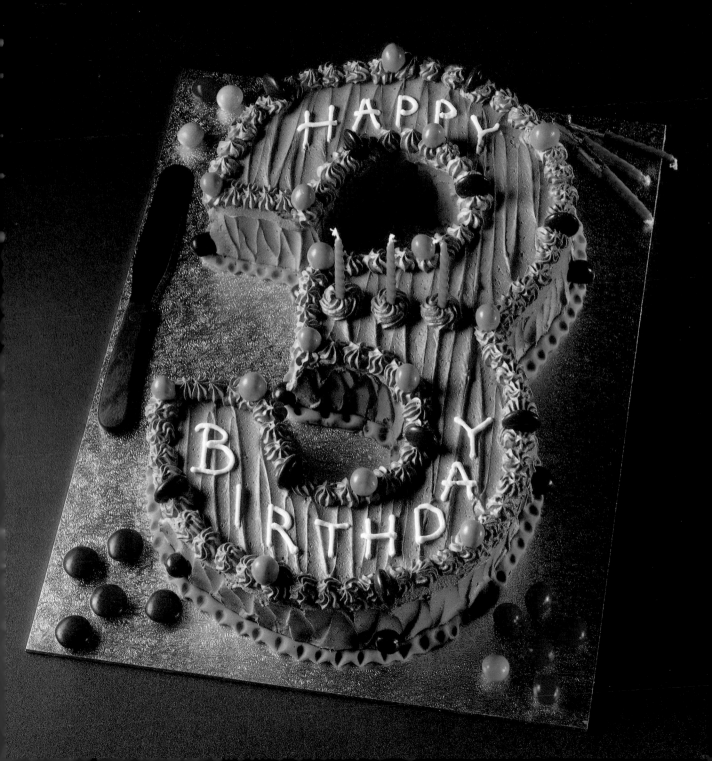

STEP 1

STEP 4

STEP 5

STEP 6

MARZIPAN & APRICOT GLAZE

Marzipan can be bought ready-made, but is easy to make yourself. This recipe also explains how to make apricot glaze and how to cover a cake with marzipan. Marzipan will keep for up to 3 days if wrapped in clingfilm (plastic wrap) and stored in a cool place.

MAKES 500 G/1 LB/4 CUPS

125 g/4 oz/¹/₂ cup caster (superfine) sugar
125 g/4 oz/1 cup icing (confectioners')
   sugar, sifted
250 g/8 oz/2 cups ground almonds
1 tsp lemon juice
few drops of almond flavouring (extract)
1 egg or 2 egg yolks

APRICOT GLAZE:
175 g/6 oz/¹/₂ cup apricot jam
2 tbsp water

1 To make the marzipan, combine the sugars and ground almonds in a bowl and make a well in the centre. Add the lemon juice, almond flavouring (extract) and sufficient egg or egg yolk to mix to a firm, manageable dough.

2 Transfer to a board dusted with icing (confectioners') sugar and knead until smooth. Do not over-knead or it will become oily.

3 At this stage, the marzipan can be coloured with liquid or paste food colourings. To get a rich, deep colour, use the paste kind, as it is more concentrated. It is essential to knead evenly to prevent the colourings being streaky.

4 To make the apricot glaze, heat the jam and water in a saucepan until the jam has melted, stirring occasionally. Press through a sieve (strainer) into a clean saucepan. Return to the boil and simmer until beginning to thicken. Cool and store in an airtight container in the refrigerator for up to a week.

5 To cover a cake with marzipan, place almost half the marzipan on a work surface (counter) dredged with icing (confectioners') sugar and roll out until 2.5 cm/1 inch larger than the top of the cake. Brush the cake top with apricot glaze, invert the cake on the marzipan and turn right way up. Trim off the excess marzipan.

6 Brush the sides of the cake with the glaze. Cut 2 pieces of string, one to match the depth of the cake, the other the circumference. Roll out the remaining marzipan to the depth and circumference of the cake, using the strings as a guide. Place the marzipan around the side of the cake, moulding it evenly. Smooth the join and store, uncovered, for 2 days for a Madeira (Pound) Cake or 4–6 days for a rich fruit cake, to set. Use any leftovers for moulding animals and figures.

BUTTER CREAM & ROYAL ICING

These are both used for decorating cakes, and butter cream is also used as a filling. They can both be coloured and butter cream can be flavoured to complement the cake.

STEP 1

BUTTER CREAM:
FILLS AND COVERS A 23 CM/9 INCH CAKE
125 g/4 oz/¹/₂ cup butter or soft margarine
175–250 g/6–8 oz/1¹/₂–2 cups icing (confectioners') sugar, sifted
1–2 tbsp milk
few drops of vanilla flavouring (extract) or other flavouring

ROYAL ICING:
MAKES 500 G/1 LB/4 CUPS
2 egg whites
500 g/1 lb/4 cups icing (confectioners') sugar, sifted
2 tsp lemon juice, strained
1 tsp glycerine (optional)

1 To make the butter cream, cream the fat until very soft and then gradually beat in enough sugar and milk to give a fairly firm but spreading consistency.

2 Beat in the vanilla flavouring (extract), and if the butter cream is not to be used at once, store in a sealed airtight container for up to a week in the refrigerator. Stir well before using.

3 For coffee butter cream, replace the milk with 2–3 teaspoons coffee

STEP 3

flavouring (extract) or instant coffee powder; for chocolate, add 30–45 g/ 1–1½ oz/1–1½ squares melted dark chocolate or 2–3 tablespoons sifted cocoa powder; for orange or lemon, omit the vanilla, replace the milk with orange or lemon juice and add the finely grated rind of 1 orange or lemon.

4 To make royal icing, put the egg whites into a clean bowl and beat until frothy. Using a wooden spoon, gradually beat in half the icing (confectioners') sugar. Add the lemon juice, glycerine, if using, and sufficient of the remaining sugar, a tablespoonful at a time, to achieve the right consistency. Beat well until the mixture is smooth, very white and stands in soft peaks.

STEP 4

5 At this stage the icing may be coloured with liquid or paste food colouring, added very sparingly with the tip of a skewer or cocktail stick (toothpick). Beat in the colour well until even.

6 Store in a sealed airtight container or cover the bowl with a damp cloth to prevent a skin forming, and preferably leave to stand for an hour or so, to allow the air bubbles to disperse.

STEP 5

STEP 2

STEP 3

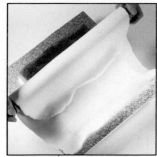

STEP 5

STEP 6

SUGARPASTE

Sugarpaste is used both to cover cakes and for moulding. It is easy to colour using a paste food colouring, but knead it in thoroughly so it is evenly mixed. Ready-made paste can be bought in supermarkets and specialist cake decorating shops.

MAKES 500 G/1 LB/4 CUPS

500 g/1 lb/4 cups icing (confectioners')
*   sugar, sifted*
1 egg white
50 ml/2 fl oz/4 tbsp liquid glucose or
*   glucose syrup*
icing (confectioners') sugar and cornflour
*   (cornstarch) to knead*
paste food colourings

1 Put the icing (confectioners') sugar in a bowl and make a well in the centre. Add the egg white and liquid glucose or glucose syrup.

2 Beat with a wooden spoon, gradually drawing in the icing (confectioners') sugar from the side of the bowl until the mixture is stiff.

3 Dip your hands in a mixture of icing (confectioners') sugar and cornflour (cornstarch), then knead the sugarpaste in a bowl, using the fingertips and kneading in a circular movement until smooth.

4 To colour the paste, add the paste food colouring sparingly from the tip of a skewer or cocktail stick (toothpick). Even deep colours need only

½–¾ teaspoon. Knead again until smooth and evenly blended. If the colour is not blended properly, it will be streaky when rolled out. Store in an airtight container or sealed thick polythene (plastic) bag for up to 2–3 days in a cool place, if it is not to be used at once.

5 To cover a cake, first brush the cake with jam or apricot glaze (see page 12). Roll out the sugarpaste on baking parchment dredged with sifted icing (confectioners') sugar so it is 13–15 cm/ 5–6 inches larger than the cake (depending on the depth of the cake). Support the sugarpaste on a rolling pin, remove from the parchment, and position centrally on top of the cake.

6 Using fingertips dipped in a mixture of icing (confectioners') sugar and cornflour (cornstarch), press the sugarpaste to fit the cake, working from the centre to the edge, then down the sides in a circular movement. Trim off the excess sugarpaste from around the base. The sides can also be smoothed with a specialist implement called a side smoother, or with a jam jar. Leave to set.

CHAPTER TWO

Butter Cream Cakes

❀

Butter cream is good for covering cakes of all sorts, as the ideas in this chapter show. It is often used in combination with sugarpaste or marzipan for both the filling and the decorations, particularly as an alternative to royal icing. The flavour of butter cream can be varied to suit the taste of the child and to complement the cake, and it can be coloured as required with either liquid or paste food colouring. It is also easy to spread and pipe.

After the cake has been cut and shaped using a template, such as an elephant, lamb or teddy bear, it should be placed on a suitably sized cake board. Next brush the cake all over with apricot glaze or sieved (strained) jam, which will make it much easier to spread or pipe the butter cream without pulling up any crumbs.

Once butter cream is made, it can be stored in the refrigerator in an airtight container for up to a week, either plain or coloured or flavoured, before use. Butter cream can also be frozen, either on the decorated cake or before it is added. If frozen, make sure it is thoroughly thawed and well blended before it is used.

Opposite: *Butter cream cakes are particularly suitable for younger children, as they are light to eat and not too sweet. They can be made in almost any shape and flavour, and in pale or bright colours.*

STEP 2

STEP 4

STEP 5

STEP 6

HAPPY LION

A smiling-faced lion made from sponge cake with a butter cream and marzipan decoration.

4-egg Victoria Sandwich (Sponge Layer
  Cake), Quick Mix Cake or Madeira
  (Pound) Cake mixture (see page 8 or 10)
4 tbsp apricot jam, sieved (strained)
350 g/12 oz/3 cups yellow marzipan or
  sugarpaste (see page 12 or 16)
yellow, brown and red liquid or paste food
  colourings
3 quantities coffee butter cream (see page
  15)
2 chocolate buttons or beans
few pieces of thin spaghetti

1 Grease and line a 23 cm/9 inch deep round cake tin (pan). Spoon in the cake mixture. Bake in a preheated oven at 160°C/325°F/Gas Mark 3, allowing about 50–60 minutes (1–1¼ hours for Quick Mix and Madeira (Pound) Cake). Invert on a wire rack and leave for 12–24 hours.

2 Using a sharp serrated knife, pare off a piece from the top edge of the cake and place it around the base, attaching with jam; then brush the whole cake with jam.

3 Cover the top of the cake with 250 g/8 oz/2 cups sugarpaste or marzipan coloured yellow. Keep the trimmings for step 6.

4 Put the butter cream into a piping bag fitted with a large star nozzle (tip) and pipe a circle of elongated stars, beginning about 2.5 cm/1 inch up the side of the cake and taking them out towards the edge of the cake board. Then pipe 2 more circles, the third row beginning about 2.5 cm/1 inch in from the top edge on the lion's face, taking it part way down the side of the cake.

5 Roll out half the remaining marzipan or sugarpaste and cut out 2 circles of about 5 cm/2 inches for the ears. Colour a scrap of the trimmings red for a mouth. Colour the remainder deep brown, roll it out and cut out 2 × 2.5 cm/ 1 inch circles. Place one in each ear circle. Cut out 2 × 4 cm/1½ inch rounds for eyes and mould the rest into a pointed nose.

6 Squeeze the base of the ears together and attach to the cake, with butter cream. Position the eyes, the mouth, the nose, and 2 wedges (made from the yellow trimmings) beneath the nose, and attach them all with butter cream. Use chocolate buttons for eyes, add a small dot of butter cream to each, then stick pieces of spaghetti into the yellow wedges for whiskers. Leave to set.

STEP 2

STEP 3

STEP 4

STEP 5

BABA THE LAMB

Butter cream and sugarpaste are used to create this woolly lamb with a black face and legs set in a meadow of flowers.

6-egg Victoria Sandwich (Sponge Layer Cake) or Madeira (Pound) Cake mixture (see page 8 or 10)
6 tbsp apricot jam, sieved (strained)
350 g/12 oz/3 cups sugarpaste (see page 16)
black, green, blue, yellow and pink liquid or paste food colourings
3 quantities vanilla-flavoured butter cream (see page 15)
few sugar mimosa balls

1 Grease and line a 30 × 25 cm/12 × 10 inch roasting tin (pan). Spread the cake mixture evenly in it. Bake in a preheated oven at 160°C/325°F/Gas Mark 3 for about 50–60 minutes (1–1¼ hours for Madeira (Pound) Cake) or until firm to the touch. Invert on a wire rack and leave to set for 12–24 hours.

2 Trim the cake and place upside-down on a cake board. Draw the shape of a lamb on a piece of stiff paper or card, cut out and position on the cake. The ears and tail can be cut from the cake trimmings. Cut round the template. Cut out and attach the ears and tail with jam. Then brush all over with jam.

3 Colour 90 g/3 oz/¾ cup of the sugarpaste green and roll out

thinly. Use to cover the board around the lamb's legs and body up to sky level, attaching with jam. Colour 60 g/2 oz/½ cup sugarpaste blue for the sky, roll out and use to cover the rest of the cake board.

4 Colour the remaining sugarpaste black or brownish-black and roll out thinly. Use to cover the head and ears of the lamb, and then the legs, pressing evenly to the cake. Trim off where it meets the grass and sky.

5 Add a touch of yellow colouring to three quarters of the butter cream. Put it into a piping bag fitted with a small star nozzle (tip) and pipe stars all over the body and tail to touch the head, legs, sky and grass. Add a small star for each eye and put a dot of black sugarpaste in the centre. Add a black sugarpaste nose.

6 Colour a tablespoon of the remaining butter cream pink, and the remainder grass green. Put both into piping bags fitted with star nozzles (tips). Pipe rough patches of grass on the cake board as in the photograph. Add stars of pink butter cream for daisies and complete with a mimosa ball.

PINKY THE ELEPHANT

This is a cheerful cake particularly suitable for a young child.

STEP 2

5-egg Victoria Sandwich (Sponge Layer Cake) or Madeira (Pound) Cake mixture, any flavour (see page 8 or 10)
4 tbsp apricot jam, sieved (strained)
3 quantities butter cream (see page 15)
pink, yellow and green liquid or paste food colourings
2 black or chocolate sweets (candies), for eyes

1 Grease and line a 25 cm/10 inch deep round cake tin (pan). Spread the cake mixture evenly in it. Bake in a preheated oven at 160°C/325°F/Gas Mark 3 for about 1 hour (1¼–1½ hours for Madeira (Pound) Cake) or until firm to the touch. Invert on a wire rack and leave to set for 12–24 hours.

2 Draw a 25 cm/10 inch circle on a piece of card and draw a pattern for the head, ears and tusks of an elephant. Cut out, position on the cake and cut out carefully.

3 Assemble the cake on a cake board, sticking together with jam. Brush the apricot jam all over the cake.

4 Colour about three-quarters of the remaining butter cream bright pink and put into a piping bag fitted with

a star nozzle (tip). Pipe either stars or lines all over the cake, including the sides, marking a defining line around the ears.

5 Colour about 4 tablespoons of the butter cream pale yellow, put into a piping bag fitted with a star nozzle (tip) and use to cover the tusks, either with stars or lines.

6 Pipe circles of cream-coloured butter cream for eyes on the head and complete with the sweets (candies).

7 Colour the remaining butter cream grass green and again using a star nozzle (tip), pipe stars or lines over the cake board to cover. Add candles if required. Leave to set.

STEP 3

STEP 4

STEP 6

STEP 2

STEP 3

STEP 4

STEP 6

TEDDY THE BEAR

*Everyone's friend, this cuddly teddy bear is covered in butter cream
which can be in any colour you like, with a bow to match.*

6-egg Victoria Sandwich (Sponge Layer
   Cake), Quick Mix Cake or Madeira
   (Pound) Cake mixture (see page 8 or 10)
6 tbsp apricot jam, sieved (strained)
3 quantities butter cream (see page 15)
5 tbsp sifted cocoa powder or brown liquid or
   paste food colouring
sweets (candies) for eyes
60 g/2 oz/$^1/_2$ cup sugarpaste (see page 16)
black and red, green or yellow liquid or paste
   food colouring

1 Grease and line a roasting tin (pan)
about 30 × 25 cm/12 × 10 inches.
Spread the cake mixture evenly in it and
bake in a preheated oven at 160°C/
325°F/Gas Mark 3 for 50–60 minutes
(1–1¼ hours for Quick Mix and Madeira
(Pound) Cake). Invert on a wire rack and
leave to set for 12–24 hours.

2 Draw a template for a teddy bear
on a piece of card, allowing enough
trimmings to make the ears, nose and
tummy. Place on the cake and cut out.
From the trimmings, cut out the ears, a
nose and a rounded tummy. Place the
cake on a board and attach the ears, nose
and tummy with jam. Then brush the
whole cake with the jam.

3 Put about one third of the butter
cream into a piping bag fitted with
a large star nozzle (tip) and pipe stars all
over the nose, paws and tummy of the
bear, reserving a little butter cream for
the ears.

4 Colour the remaining butter cream
brown with the cocoa powder or
brown food colouring. Put into a piping
bag fitted with a large star nozzle (tip)
and pipe curved lines all over the head,
tummy, ears and paws of the bear,
making sure the butter cream reaches
down the sides of the cake.

5 Use the reserved butter cream to
pipe the centres of the ears. Add
sweets (candies) for the bear's eyes and
nose.

6 Colour a scrap of sugarpaste black,
roll into very thin sausages and use
to complete the bear's nose and mouth
and claws to the tips of the paws. Colour
the remaining sugarpaste a bright colour
and use to make a bow to place around
the bear's neck. Leave to set.

BEAUTIFUL BUTTERFLY

A pretty cake with delicate colourings and flavourings. The colourings could be made darker and more dramatic, of course, if you think your child would prefer a different kind of butterfly.

STEP 3

STEP 4

STEP 5

STEP 6

4-egg Victoria Sandwich (Sponge Layer
   Cake) mixture, any flavour (see page 8)
3 quantities butter cream (see page 15)
4 tbsp apricot jam, sieved (strained)
pink and purple liquid or paste food
   colourings
scarlet balls
candles and holders (optional)

1 Grease and line the base of 2 × 23 cm/9 inch round sandwich tins (layer pans). Divide the cake mixture between the tins (pans) and bake in a preheated oven at 180°C/350°F/Gas Mark 4 for about 30–35 minutes, or until firm to the touch. Invert on a wire rack and leave to set for 12–24 hours.

2 Use a little of the butter cream to sandwich the 2 cakes together, then cut the cake evenly in half. If liked, a small dip can be cut out of the base of each wing.

3 Position the 2 halves back to back on a cake board at a slightly slanting angle so the wings are wider apart at the top. Brush all over with apricot jam.

4 Colour about two thirds of the butter cream pale pink and spread all over the cake. Using a serrated icing (frosting) comb or fork, mark wavy lines around the sides of the cake.

5 Tint some of the remaining butter cream mauve. Put it into a piping bag fitted with a small star nozzle (tip) and pipe a shell outline around the top and base of the butterfly. Then divide each wing in half by piping shapes about 2 cm/¾ inch in from the edge of the cake and pipe a wavy line between the wings to make a body.

6 Put the remaining butter cream into a piping bag fitted with a fairly fine writing nozzle (tip). Use to pipe wavy lace patterns on the butterfly wings.

7 Add scarlet balls to complete the decoration of the butterfly. If liked, add candles in holders for the antennae. Leave to set.

VARIATION

Other colour schemes for the butterfly could include shades of yellow and orange; green and cream; or pink and blue.

CHAPTER THREE

Sports & Games

❀

This section covers cakes to suit many different activities enjoyed by a wide variety of children, both boys and girls. Whether your child loves horse-riding or swimming or indoor pursuits like board games, there are ideas to cover all these interests, and many more. Each of the cakes can then be personalized by adding the name of the child, candles if required, and perhaps using the colour of the child's favourite pony or team. The scene around the actual cake can be made even more realistic by decorating it in a variety of different coloured icings (frostings) with a wide selection of piping nozzles (tips) – for instance the garden scene around the swimming pool, and hedges, fence and trees around the pony.

These cakes can be made in any flavour you like and are mainly covered in sugarpaste, and decorated with either butter cream or royal icing. Royal icing is best made the day before to allow time for the air bubbles to come to the surface and burst, thus preventing bubbles when it is piped.

While the piping bags are waiting to be used, keep them wrapped in a polythene (plastic) bag so the icing (frosting) doesn't dry out.

Opposite: *Children's cakes can be made for any celebration, and not just for their birthday – a brightly coloured cake will be welcome on any occasion, from Easter to Christmas.*

STEP 3

STEP 4

STEP 5

STEP 6

RACING CAR

Racing cars come in all shapes and sizes, are usually brightly coloured and can be traditional or modern. Shape the cake to the design of the car you like best, or make it similar to the family car, if preferred.

2 × 3-egg Quick Mix Cake or Madeira
   (Pound) Cake mixture, any flavour (see
   page 8 or 10)
6 tbsp apricot jam, sieved (strained)
1 kg/2 lb/8 cups sugarpaste (see page 16)
blue and black liquid or paste food colourings
250 g/8 oz/2 cups royal icing (see page 15)
4 wooden cocktail sticks (toothpicks) or
   plastic skewers

1 Grease 2 roasting tins (pans) 28 × 18 × 4 cm/11 × 7 × 1½ inches, and line with baking parchment. Spread the cake mixture evenly in the tins (pans). Bake in a preheated oven at 160°C/325°F/Gas Mark 3 for about 45–50 minutes until firm. Invert on wire racks and leave to set for 12–24 hours.

2 Trim the cakes to a width of 11 cm/ 4½ inches wide, reserving the trimmings. Sandwich the cakes together with jam. Slightly taper one end of the cake and round the other end for the back of the car. About 10 cm/4 inches from the back of the car cut out a wedge through the top layer of cake for the seat. Use a piece of the cake trimmings to build up the car behind the seat. Add a small elongated triangular piece of cake to the top of the bonnet (hood), attaching all with jam.

3 From the other trimmings, cut out 2 wheels of 5 cm/2 inches and 2 of 6 cm/2½ inches. The larger back wheels should be wider than the front ones. Brush the car and tyres with jam.

4 Colour 625 g/1¼ lb/5 cups of the sugarpaste bright blue. Roll out and use to cover the entire car, moulding to fit all the undulations, but cutting out a piece for the seat so it does not split.

5 Colour 250 g/8 oz/2 cups of the sugarpaste black. Roll out and use a piece to fit inside the seat area of the car, and to cover the tyres. Mark treads on the tyres with a sharp knife, then attach with cocktail sticks (toothpicks) and a dab of royal icing. Also mould a steering wheel, an anti-roll bar to put behind the seat, and 2 wing mirrors, and attach.

6 Colour the remaining sugarpaste grey, and use for a seat in the car, a front radiator, and trims to the wheels. Colour the royal icing grey and using a No 2 writing nozzle (tip), pipe spokes on the tyres and a radiator grille on the car. Pipe the age of the child for the car number and, if liked, a name or message on the car or board. Leave to set.

STEP 4

STEP 5

STEP 5

STEP 6

MY PONY

An ideal cake for a child who is mad about horses. Simply find out the colour of his or her favourite pony and make the icing (frosting) the same colour.

6-egg chocolate-flavoured Victoria Sandwich (Sponge Layer Cake) or Quick Mix Cake mixture (see page 8)
6 tbsp apricot jam, sieved (strained)
875 g/1¾ lb/7 cups sugarpaste (see page 16)
green, blue, black and brown liquid or paste food colouring
1 quantity butter cream (see page 15)
few long chocolate matchsticks

1 Grease and line a roasting tin (pan) 30 × 25 cm/12 × 10 inches. Spread the cake mixture evenly in it. Bake in a preheated oven at 160°C/325°F/Gas Mark 3 for about 50–60 minutes (1–1¼ hours for Quick Mix Cake). Invert on a wire rack and leave to set for 24 hours.

2 Trim the cake, place upside-down on a cake board and brush all over with the apricot jam. Colour 250 g/8 oz/ 2 cups of the sugarpaste sky blue, roll out and lay over the top third of the cake, giving it a slightly uneven edge. Trim off around the base neatly.

3 Colour about 425 g/14 oz/3½ cups of the sugarpaste grass green. Roll out and use to cover the rest of the cake, matching it evenly to the sky, and trim off neatly around the base.

4 Draw a picture of a horse on thick paper or card and cut out. Colour about 175 g/6 oz/1½ cups of the sugarpaste the colour of the pony and roll it out large enough to place the template on. Cut carefully around the template. Remove the template carefully and then even more carefully move the horse to the top of the cake, dampening in places so it will stick.

5 Roll out the trimmings and make a mane, tail and forelock, marking with a knife to make it look realistic. Mark in the eyes, nostrils and mouth with a cocktail stick (toothpick). Place the chocolate matchsticks on the cake to form a fence, attaching with butter cream.

6 Colour the butter cream grass green and put into a piping bag fitted with a star nozzle (tip). Pipe squiggly lines to make a hedge at each end of the fence plus a couple of trees (adding chocolate matchsticks for trunks). Use the remaining butter cream to pipe uneven lengths of grass up the sides of the cake to attach to the board, and random patches of grass on the cake.

FOOTBALL

This cake can be made in a special round cake mould or by using two basins, and can be decorated differently – as a basketball, for example – to suit the interest of the child. The colours of the scarf should, of course, match the child's favourite team.

4-egg Madeira (Pound) Cake mixture (see page 10)
1 quantity butter cream (see page 15)
4 tbsp jam, sieved (strained)
1 kg/2 lb/8 cups sugarpaste (see page 16)
black, blue and deep red liquid or paste food colouring

1 Grease the 2 separate halves of a spherical Christmas pudding mould, about 12.5 cm/5 inches in diameter, or 2 basins of 900 ml/1½ pints/3¾ cups capacity. Place pieces of baking parchment in the base of each and dredge lightly with flour. Place the containers level on baking sheets, holding in place with foil or in another basin to keep them from tipping over.

2 Divide the cake mixture between the containers, filling no more than three quarters full and levelling the tops. Bake in a preheated oven at 160°C/325°F/Gas Mark 3 for about 1–1½ hours until firm to the touch. Invert on a wire rack and leave to set for 12–24 hours.

3 Trim the cakes evenly and sandwich together with most of the butter cream. Then cut off a slice from the base so that the ball will stand upright, and place the football on a cake

STEP 3

board, attaching with butter cream. Brush all over with jam.

4 Roll out about 625 g/1¼ lb/5 cups sugarpaste and use to cover the ball, moulding carefully to fit. Colour half the remaining sugarpaste black, roll out and cut into hexagons, about 5 cm/2 inches across.

5 Attach the hexagons evenly all over the football, by dampening slightly, so they stick and just touch. Leave to set.

6 Colour most of the remaining sugarpaste deep maroon and the rest pale blue. Roll out the maroon sugarpaste to make a scarf, then roll out the pale blue and add for a fringe and stripes. Lay the scarf around the base of the football, as if abandoned.

7 Use the remaining butter cream to write 'Happy Birthday' either on the board or the cake. Leave to set.

STEP 4

STEP 5

STEP 6

STEP 3

STEP 4

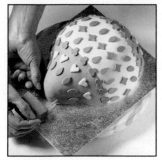

STEP 5

STEP 6

HOT AIR BALLOON

A pretty, brightly coloured large hot air balloon with a basket underneath it, decorated all over with sugarpaste or marzipan shapes.

4-egg Victoria Sandwich (Sponge Layer Cake), Quick Mix Cake or Madeira (Pound) Cake mixture (see page 8 or 10)
6 tbsp apricot jam, sieved (strained)
1 kg/ 2 lb/ 8 cups sugarpaste or marzipan (see page 12 or 16)
yellow, orange, green and mauve liquid or paste food colourings
1 quantity butter cream (see page 15)
4 wooden skewers

1 Grease a 23 cm/9 inch bowl (about 2.25 litres/4 pints/2½ quart capacity) thoroughly. Spoon the cake mixture into the bowl, making sure it is evenly distributed, and level the top. Bake in a preheated oven at 160°C/ 325°F/Gas Mark 3 for about 1¼–1½ hours until firm to the touch and a skewer inserted in the centre comes out clean. Invert on a wire rack and leave to set for 24 hours.

2 Place the cake upside-down on a rectangular cake board and brush all over with the jam. Take about 125 g/ 4 oz/1 cup of the sugarpaste or marzipan and mould a piece to put at the base of the balloon to make it elongated.

3 Colour about 175 g/6 oz/1½ cups of the sugarpaste or marzipan

mauve, then divide the remainder into 3 pieces and colour them yellow, orange and green respectively. Roll out about three quarters of each of the 3 large pieces of sugarpaste or marzipan and use each to form a wide stripe around the balloon, so it is completely covered.

4 Shape 125 g/4 oz/1 cup of the mauve sugarpaste or marzipan into a small rectangle for the basket. Cut out various shapes in the different colours of sugarpaste or marzipan with a cutter or a sharp knife and attach them in even bands to the balloon to make it as pretty and vibrant as possible.

5 Attach the rectangular piece of sugarpaste or marzipan for the basket at the base of the balloon and stick the skewers into the basket and the base of the balloon to represent the ropes, as shown.

6 Colour half the butter cream green and the remainder orange. Put into piping bags fitted with small star nozzles (tips) and use to decorate both the basket and the balloon. Use a spare piece of green sugarpaste to make a banner and pipe on a message with the buttercream, if liked. Leave to set.

STEP 2

STEP 4

STEP 5

STEP 6

SWIMMING POOL

An amusing cake to make in any flavour, suitable for a summer party and for a child of any age.

5-egg and 2-egg Victoria Sandwich (Sponge Layer Cake) mixture (see page 8)
1 quantity butter cream (see page 15)
6 tbsp apricot jam, sieved (strained)
1 kg/2 lb/8 cups sugarpaste (see page 16)
blue, green, pink, brown and orange liquid or paste food colourings

1 Grease and line a roasting tin (pan) about 30 × 25 cm/12 × 10 inches and another of 28 × 18 × 4 cm/11 × 7 × 1½ inches. Spread the 5-egg mixture in the larger tin (pan) and the 2-egg one in the smaller tin (pan). Bake in a preheated oven at 180°C/350°F/Gas Mark 4 until firm to the touch: about 50 minutes for the larger cake and 25 minutes for the smaller. Invert on wire racks and leave to set for 12–24 hours.

2 Place the large cake on a cake board. Trim the other cake and attach on top of the larger cake at the back with butter cream. Brush the whole cake with jam.

3 Colour 175 g/6 oz/1½ cups sugarpaste blue. Roll out and cover the top of the raised part of the cake. Colour 500 g/1 lb/4 cups sugarpaste green. Roll out some of it and use to cover the rest of the cake and up the sides

of the pool just overlapping the blue sugarpaste. Trim off around the base.

4 Roll out 90 g/3 oz/¾ cup of white sugarpaste and cut into 2 cm/¾ inch wide strips. Dampen and attach around the top edge of the pool, Mark at intervals to represent paving stones.

5 Colour 125 g/4 oz/1 cup of sugarpaste pale pink and use to make the top half of 3 bodies, and a body to sit on the side of the pool. Using a fine paintbrush and food colouring, paint on hair and other details. Leave to dry and position in the pool. Colour the rest of the sugarpaste in bright colours and shape into 2 or 3 towels, to throw on the grass.

6 Shape the remaining green sugarpaste into trees and place around the pool. Colour a tiny amount of butter cream pink and put into a piping bag fitted with a star nozzle (tip). Colour the remaining butter cream green and put into a piping bag fitted with a star or thick writing nozzle (tip). Pipe grass around the sides of the cake, working up from the board; and pipe patches of grass on the cake and around the edge of the pool. Add flowers by piping pink stars of icing (frosting) here and there.

STEP 2

STEP 4

STEP 5

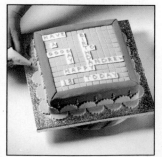

STEP 6

CROSSWORD PUZZLE

The message on this attractive cake can be worked out to suit any occasion and the flavourings and colourings altered likewise.

4-egg Victoria Sandwich (Sponge Layer Cake), Quick Mix Cake or Madeira (Pound) Cake mixture (see page 8 or 10)
6 tbsp apricot jam, sieved (strained)
875 g/1³⁄₄ lb/7 cups sugarpaste (see page 16)
blue, green and orange liquid or paste food colourings
250 g/8 oz/2 cups royal icing (see page 15)

1 Grease and line a 23 cm/9 inch deep square cake tin (pan). Spread the cake mixture evenly in it. Bake in a preheated oven at 160°C/325°F/Gas Mark 3 for 50–60 minutes (1–1¼ hours for Quick Mix and Madeira (Pound) Cake). Invert on a wire rack and leave to set for 12–24 hours. Stand the cake upside-down on a 30 cm/12 inch cake board. Brush all over carefully with the apricot jam. Colour 500 g/1 lb/4 cups of the sugarpaste mid blue. Colour 300 g/ 10 oz/2½ cups of the sugarpaste deep green and leave the remainder white.

2 Roll out three quarters of the blue sugarpaste and use to cover the top of the cake. Mark the sugarpaste into a crossword design of 12 lines each way but leaving a margin of about 1 cm/ ½ inch all round the edge. This should give 12 squares down and across.

3 Cut a piece of string long enough to reach round the outside of the cake, then cut the string in half. Roll out the deep green sugarpaste to the depth of the cake plus about 1 cm/½ inch. Cut out 2 strips the length of each piece of string. Place around the sides of the cake, bending the overlap over the top edge of the cake to reach the crossword, trimming the corners as necessary.

4 Roll out the remaining blue sugarpaste. Cut into 4 cm/1½ inch circles, flute the edges and then cut each of these in half. Attach around the base of the cake with a dab of apricot jam.

5 Roll out the white sugarpaste and cut into strips the width of the squares on the crossword. Position to make your message look like words in a crossword, then mark each with a knife.

6 Colour the royal icing orange and put a little into a piping bag fitted with a No. 2 writing nozzle (tip). Use to fill in the letters. Put the remaining royal icing in a piping bag fitted with a star nozzle (tip) and pipe a star decoration around the base. Complete the decoration with stars and dots of royal icing as shown.

CRICKET BAT

Just the cake to give a sporty-minded child for a birthday, particularly if he or she is keen on cricket. You can copy the markings from a real bat.

5-egg Victoria Sandwich (Sponge Layer
  Cake) or Madeira (Pound) Cake mixture,
  any flavour (see page 8 or 10)
2 quantities butter cream (see page 15)
5 tbsp apricot jam, sieved (strained)
1 kg/2 lb/8 cups sugarpaste (see page 16)
brown, red, yellow, black and green liquid or
  paste food colourings

1 Grease and line a roasting tin (pan) about 30 × 25 cm/12 × 10 inches. Spread the cake mixture in the tin (pan), making sure there is plenty of mixture in the corners. Bake in a preheated oven at 160°C/325°F/Gas Mark 3 for about 50 minutes (1–1¼ hours for Madeira (Pound) Cake) until well risen and firm to the touch. Invert on a wire rack and leave to set for 12–24 hours.

2 Cut a 2.5 cm/1 inch slice off one narrow end, halve this and sandwich together with butter cream for the handle. Cut the rest of the cake in half lengthways and sandwich together with butter cream. Round one end and cut away a slightly slanting slice towards the centre of the cake on the long sides; place on a cake board.

3 Brush the cake all over with the jam. Colour 625 g/1¼ lb/5 cups

sugarpaste light brown. Roll out and use to cover the cricket bat completely, trimming off around the base.

4 Colour the remaining sugarpaste deep red. Use some of it to cover the 'handle' of the bat after brushing with jam and position at the top of the bat. Roll out a tiny piece for a deep triangle to place at the top of the bat where it meets the handle.

5 Roll the remaining red sugarpaste into a cricket ball and mark the seams with the back of a knife, as in the photograph. Place beside the bat. Using some butter cream in a piping bag fitted with a fine writing nozzle (tip), pipe small lines around the ball for the markings.

6 Write your message and the name of the child down the length of the bat. Colour the remaining butter cream green and put into a piping bag fitted with a star nozzle (tip). Pipe green stars all over the board to represent grass. Leave to set.

STEP 3

STEP 4

STEP 5

STEP 6

SNAKES & LADDERS CAKE

This is a very popular game which can be played by the children at the party before the cake is cut.

5-egg quantity Victoria Sandwich (Sponge Layer Cake) or Madeira (Pound) Cake mixture, any flavour (see page 8 or 10)
5 tbsp apricot jam, sieved (strained)
1 kg/2 lb/8 cups sugarpaste (see page 16)
green, blue, yellow, red, orange and black liquid or paste food colourings
1 quantity royal icing (see page 15)

1 Grease and line a 25 cm/10 inch square cake tin (pan). Spread the cake mixture evenly in it. Bake in a preheated oven at 160°C/325°F/Gas Mark 3 for about 1–1¼ hours, or until firm to the touch. Invert on a wire rack and leave to set for 12–24 hours.

2 Trim the cake and place upside-down on a cake board. Brush all over with jam.

3 Colour about 750 g/1½ lb/6 cups of the sugarpaste green and use to cover the whole cake, trimming off evenly around the base. Using the back of a knife, mark the top of the cake into 2 cm/¾ inch squares. Leave to set.

4 Colour about 60 g/2 oz/½ cup each of the sugarpaste red, blue and yellow, and shape these into snakes of various lengths. Place them on the board as in the photograph. Also shape 4 round counters about 1 cm/½ inch across, and colour each one a different colour, either red, blue, yellow or white.

5 Colour about half the royal icing pale green, put into a piping bag fitted with a writing nozzle (tip) and pipe numbers on all the squares; then, using a star nozzle (tip), pipe a decoration around the base of the cake with alternate stars and elongated stars. Add loops from star to star with the writing nozzle (tip).

6 Colour the remaining royal icing orange and put into a piping bag fitted with a fairly thick writing nozzle (tip). Pipe ladders on the cake as in the photograph. Finally, use the remaining sugarpaste to make into square dice; add tiny dots of black food colouring to complete the dice.

VARIATION

The colour scheme of this cake can be changed to suit your taste. Try a basic colouring of red, blue or yellow.

CHAPTER FOUR

Party Cakes

❦

Party cakes can be made to cover a wide variety of parties and to suit many tastes and age groups. A younger child will appreciate the Panda's Picnic or Tortoise, while an older child might prefer the bath, particularly if he or she is someone who likes to lounge in the bath for hours on end listening to the radio! A Boat Cake may bring back happy memories of family holidays and the Clown remind you of a fancy dress party or the circus. Most novelty cakes will take quite a time to prepare and decorate. It is no good thinking it can be done in half an hour or so; always allow plenty of time first to make the cake and leave it to rest for at least twelve hours, then to prepare the icing (frosting) and colour the sugarpaste – and that's in addition to the actual assembling and decoration itself. You must also allow time for the cake to set after the decoration has been completed, so it is best to arrange for it to be finished two or three days before the party.

Where cakes are decorated with moulded animals or other shapes, it is best to make these at least three or four days before adding them to the cake, to give them time to dry, otherwise they may mark the cake, particularly animals such as the panda, which is made with black sugarpaste. They can be made several weeks in advance and dried, and they will then keep almost indefinitely.

Opposite: *Above all, party cakes should be fun – so don't hold back on the decoration.*

STEP 2

STEP 3

STEP 4

STEP 6

CLARENCE THE CLOWN

A cheerful cake for either a boy or a girl; the colourings can be changed to fit the colour scheme of the party or to suit your taste, as can the clown's expression.

6-egg Madeira (Pound) Cake mixture (see page 10)
6 tbsp apricot jam, sieved (strained)
1.25 kg /2½ lb/10 cups sugarpaste (see page 16)
red, orange, black, yellow and blue liquid or paste food colourings
500 g/1 lb/4 cups royal icing (see page 15) or 1½ quantities butter cream (see page 15)

1 Grease and line a 30 × 25 cm/12 × 10 inch roasting tin (pan). Spread the cake mixture evenly in it. Bake in a preheated oven at 160°C/325°F/Gas Mark 3 for 1–1¼ hours. Invert on a wire rack and leave for 12–24 hours.

2 Make a template for the clown and cut out the shape carefully. Cut out the arms and hat from the trimmings. Place the cake upside-down on a cake board and brush all over with jam.

3 Colour 175 g/6 oz/1½ cups of the sugarpaste flesh pink. Roll out and use some of it to cover the head of the clown. Mould the remainder into 2 ears and attach to the head. Colour 125 g/ 4 oz/1 cup of the sugarpaste black. Reserve a scrap for the eyes and mould the remainder into 2 feet.

4 Colour 625 g/1¼ lb/5 cups sugarpaste orange. Roll out and use to cover the clown's body, arms and hat. Dampen the arms and attach to the body. Use about 90 g/3 oz/¾ cup white sugarpaste to mould into hands and attach to the arms. Colour 90 g/3 oz/¾ cup of the sugarpaste blue and cut out shapes to stick all over the body and hat.

5 Colour 60 g/2 oz/½ cup sugarpaste bright yellow. Roll out and make into a large bow tie. Roll out most of the rest of the white sugarpaste and cut ovals for eyes and mouth, and circles for spots on face. Dampen and attach. Use the rest of the black sugarpaste for the centres of the eyes. Colour the remaining scraps of white sugarpaste red and use for a nose, mouth and eyebrows.

6 Colour two thirds of the royal icing or butter cream bright blue and the remainder yellow. Put into piping bags, the blue fitted with a star nozzle (tip) and the yellow with a thick writing nozzle (tip). Pipe a heavy blue ruff around the neck, cuffs and feet of the clown. Pipe yellow strands of hair at the back of the head. Attach the feet, bow tie and hat, and leave to set.

STEP 3

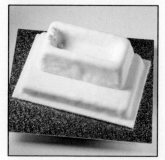

STEP 3

STEP 5

STEP 6

LUXURY BATH

For any child who spend lots of time relaxing in a bath, this will be a good reminder!

3-egg and 2-egg Victoria Sandwich (Sponge Layer Cake) or Madeira (Pound) Cake mixture, any flavour (see page 8 or 10)
5 tbsp apricot jam, sieved (strained)
625 g / 1¼ lb / 5 cups sugarpaste (see page 16)
blue and yellow liquid or paste food colourings
250 g / 8 oz / 2 cups royal icing (see page 15) or 1 quantity butter cream (see page 15)

1 Grease and line a 28 × 18 × 4 cm/ 11 × 7 × 1½ inch cake tin (pan) and a 23 × 13 cm/9 × 5 inch loaf tin (pan). Spread the 3-egg cake mixture evenly in the rectangular tin (pan) and the 2-egg mixture in the loaf tin (pan). Bake the larger cake in a preheated oven at 160°C/325°F/Gas Mark 3 for about 45–50 minutes; and the smaller cake for about 35–40 minutes. Invert on wire racks and leave to set for 12–24 hours.

2 Place the rectangular cake upside-down on a cake board and brush with jam. Roll out about 250 g/8 oz/2 cups of sugarpaste and use to cover the cake, trimming off evenly at the base.

3 Turn the loaf cake upside-down and scoop out the centre so it represents a bath. Trim the base evenly

and brush all over with jam. Roll out about 250 g/8 oz/2 cups of sugarpaste and use to cover the bath, carefully moulding it to fit the curves. Trim off around the base and place on the rectangular cake. Mould taps (faucets) from the trimmings and attach to the bath. Add a plug and overflow outlet.

4 Colour about 60 g/2 oz/½ cup of the sugarpaste trimmings yellow and use to mould 3 or 4 ducks for the bath, and a pair of slippers.

5 Colour the remaining sugarpaste 2 shades of blue. Roll out about 60 g/2 oz/½ cup of the darker blue sugarpaste to make a towel, add a fringe of the paler blue, and drape over the bath. Make a pale blue bath mat, adding a fringe of dark blue and a couple of dark blue stripes. A few stripes may be added to the towel, if liked.

6 Colour the royal icing pale blue. Using a piping bag fitted with a star nozzle (tip), pipe stars around the base of the bath and the cake to attach it to the board. Place the ducks and slippers in position. Leave to set.

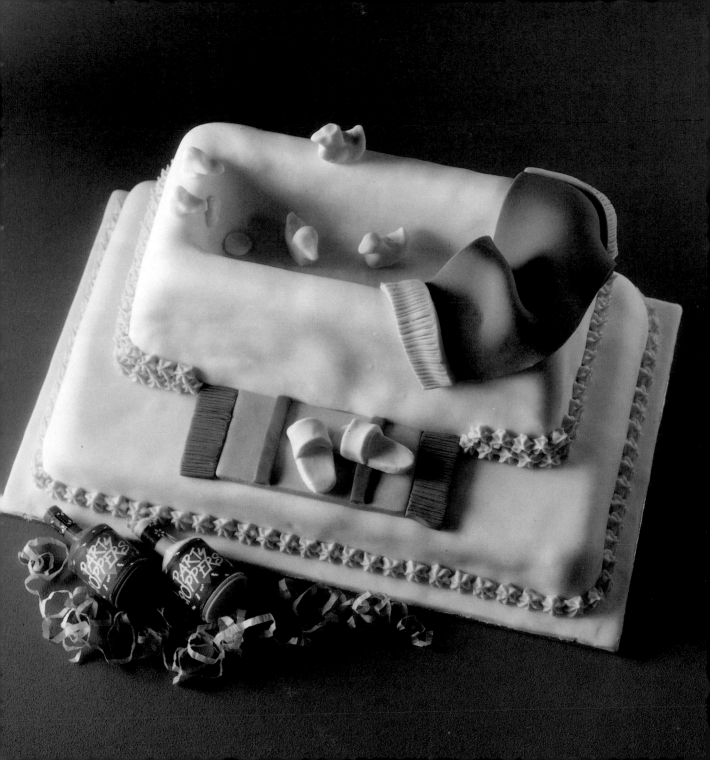

STEP 3

STEP 4

STEP 5

STEP 6

OPEN BOOK

Any book can be featured in this way – simply choose the favourite of the moment and re-create it in cake and icing (frosting).

6-egg Victoria Sandwich (Sponge Layer Cake), Quick Mix Cake or Madeira (Pound) Cake mixture (see page 8 or 10)
5 tbsp apricot jam, sieved (strained)
1.25 kg/2½ lb/10 cups sugarpaste (see page 16)
yellow, red, pink, green and orange liquid or paste food colourings
250 g/8 oz/2 cups royal icing (see page 15) or 1 quantity butter cream (see page 15)
about 50 cm/20 inches 2.5 cm/1 inch wide satin ribbon
moulded and piped bells and shells (see page 78)

1 Grease and line a roasting tin (pan) about 30 × 25 cm/12 × 10 inches. Spread the cake mixture evenly in it. Bake in a preheated oven at 160°C/ 325°F/Gas Mark 3 for 50–60 minutes. Invert on a wire rack and leave to set for 12–24 hours.

2 Place the cake upside-down on a cake board. Cut out a rounded strip down the centre of the cake, turn it upside-down and place on the right-hand page. Brush all over with jam.

3 Colour about 625 g/1¼ lb/5 cups of the sugarpaste with yellow colouring to turn it cream. Roll out most

of it and use to cover the cake so it looks like a book. Trim off around the base. Using a sharp knife, make cuts into the sides of the cake so they look like pages.

4 Roll out the rest of the cream sugarpaste to a 'page' half the size of the cake. Attach down the centre and fold it so the edge is slightly ruffled up.

5 Colour the rest of the sugarpaste red. Roll out, cut into narrow strips and place around the base of the cake to represent the book's cover. Leave to set.

6 Colour the royal icing or butter cream deep pink and put into a piping bag fitted with a writing nozzle (tip). On the left-hand page print 'Mary, Mary, Quite Contrary', keeping it to the top of the page. On the other page write some of the rhyme.

7 Using the remaining sugarpaste and royal icing or butter cream, mould and pipe some tiny bells and shells in various colours and arrange along the bottom of the page for a garden, together with green royal icing or butter cream stems and leaves, and a sugarpaste watering can. Place the ribbon down the centre of the pages as a bookmark.

TOMMY TORTOISE

A lovable pet is transformed into a cake to thrill his owner, but the colour is much brighter than usual!

4-egg Victoria Sandwich (Sponge Layer Cake) or Quick Mix Cake (see page 8)
4 tbsp apricot jam, sieved (strained)
500 g/1 lb/4 cups sugarpaste (see page16)
green, blue and brown food colouring
1 quantity butter cream (see page 15)
few sugarpaste flowers (see page 79)

1 Grease a 1.5 litre/3 pint/6 cup bowl (about 23 cm/9 inches in diameter) thoroughly and put a disc of baking parchment in the base. Add the cake mixture and bake in a preheated oven at 160°C/325°F/Gas Mark 3 for 1¼–1½ hours until well risen and firm. Cool briefly in the bowl. Invert on a wire rack and leave to set for 12–24 hours.

2 Place the cake upside-down on a cake board and trim 2.5 cm/1 inch from each side to make the tortoise oval. Cut a small V from the front for the head and 2 Vs on each side for the feet, then brush the cake all over with jam.

3 Colour 125 g/4 oz/1 cup sugarpaste greenish brown. Use one third of it to mould into a head with a thick neck and press into the head cavity. Mark 2 deep eyes, nostrils and a mouth with a skewer. Divide the remaining sugarpaste into 4 and shape into feet.

Position and then mark 4 toes on each foot with the back of a knife.

4 Colour the remaining sugarpaste green. Roll out to an oval that is large enough to cover the cake. Lift carefully and position over the cake. Make cuts over the feet and around the head, then trim so it just overlaps on to the board. Carefully mould the edges of the shell so it becomes thinner and also turn it up slightly. Place a strip of rolled paper towel under it, so it cannot fall back again. Leave until quite set.

5 Using a fairly blunt skewer, mark uneven circles, squares and other shapes all over the shell so they all touch and make a pattern as on a real tortoise. Colour about a quarter of the butter cream greenish brown and put into a piping bag fitted with a No. 2 or 3 writing nozzle (tip). Pipe a spiral inside each of the marked shapes on the tortoise.

6 Colour the remaining butter cream pale green and put into a piping bag fitted with a star nozzle (tip). Pipe stars all over the board to represent grass. Add the sugarpaste flowers to the grass. Leave to set.

HOUSE BOAT

The perfect cake for any child who loves messing about in boats. You can adapt the basic design into other kinds of boat.

STEP 2

STEP 3

STEP 4

STEP 7

6-egg Victoria Sandwich (Sponge Layer
    Cake) mixture or Madeira (Pound) Cake
    mixture (see page 8 or 10)
8 tbsp apricot jam, sieved (strained)
1.25 kg/2½ lb/10 cups sugarpaste (see
    page 16)
red, blue, black and yellow liquid or paste
    food colourings
250 g/8 oz/2 cups royal icing (see page 15)

1 Grease and line a 30 × 25 cm/12 ×
10 inch roasting tin (pan). Spread
the cake mixture evenly in it. Bake in a
preheated oven at 160°C/325°F/Gas
Mark 3 for 50–60 minutes (1–1¼ hours
for Madeira (Pound) Cake) until firm.
Invert on a wire rack and leave to set for
12–24 hours.

2 Trim the cake neatly, then cut in
half lengthways so one piece is
about 2.5 cm/1 inch wider than the
other. Slightly round one end of the
larger piece for the stern and place on a
cake board. Cut 7 cm/3 inches off the
other piece of cake and cut this piece to a
point for the bow of the barge. Attach
with jam. Brush the cake all over with
jam. Use 125 g/4 oz/1 cup of sugarpaste
to build up the bow so it is higher than
the rest.

3 Colour 750 g/1½ lb/6 cups of the
sugarpaste bright red; roll out part
of it and use to cover the whole of the
base of the barge, pressing it evenly to fit.

4 Colour 300 g/10 oz/2½ cups of the
sugarpaste deep blue and the rest
pale grey. Attach the other piece of cake
on the barge at the stern end with jam,
and brush all over with jam. Roll out the
blue sugarpaste and use to cover the
sides of the cabin. Dampen and attach
the rest around the base of the barge.

5 Roll out the remaining red sugarpaste and make a roof for the cabin,
with an attractive edging, as shown.

6 Roll out the grey sugarpaste and
cut out 4 long windows for the
sides of the cabin and 1 shorter (for the
stern end) and a door. Attach with jam.

7 Colour the royal icing yellow and
put some into a piping bag fitted
with a No. 2 writing nozzle (tip). Pipe a
decoration around the sides of the barge,
and between the windows. Pipe the
child's name on the bows. Use the rest of
the royal icing to write your message on
the roof. White sugarpaste lifebelts can
also be added.

STEP 3

STEP 4

STEP 5

STEP 5

PANDA'S PICNIC

A pretty round cake set out with a picnic on a tablecloth surrounded by moulded pandas.

4-egg Madeira (Pound) Cake or Quick Mix
  Cake mixture (see page 8 or 10)
5 tbsp apricot jam, sieved (strained)
1.5 kg/3 lb/12 cups sugarpaste (see page
  16)
green, black, orange, yellow, blue and brown
  liquid or paste food colourings
red icing (frosting) pen
1 quantity butter cream (see page 15)

1 Grease and line a 23 cm/9 inch deep round cake tin (pan). Spread the cake mixture evenly in it. Bake in a preheated oven at 160°C/325°F/Gas Mark 3 for about 1–1¼ hours, or until firm. Invert on a wire rack and leave to set for 12–24 hours. Trim the cake and place upside-down on a 28 cm/11 inch cake board. Brush all over with the jam.

2 Colour 625 g/1¼ lb/5 cups of the sugarpaste green. Roll out and use to cover the cake. Trim around the base.

3 Colour 90 g/3 oz/¾ cup of the sugarpaste pale yellow and another 90 g/3 oz/¾ cup orange. Roll them out separately and cut each into 18 pieces, 2.5 cm/1 inch square. Arrange the coloured squares alternately on the grass to make a square tablecloth, dampening each slightly so they stick.

4 Colour 375 g/12 oz/3 cups of the sugarpaste black and leave 175 g/6 oz/1½ cups of the sugarpaste white for the pandas. Make 6 pandas (see page 78–9). Each panda needs about 90 g/3 oz/¾ cup sugarpaste. Leave to dry.

5 Colour about 90 g/3 oz/¾ cup of the sugarpaste bright blue. Roll out thinly and cut out 3 plates of about 4 cm/1½ inches and 6 of 2 cm/¾ inch. Using a finger, press into the plates to give a rim. Mould 6 cups or mugs out of the trimmings. Roll out a little of the white sugarpaste and cut into sandwiches. Draw around the sides with an icing (frosting) pen for the filling and place on one of the large plates. Colour the rest of the sugarpaste brown and shape into a round or loaf cake. Cut or slice and put some pieces on the small plates. Arrange the plates and mugs on the tablecloth, dampening to attach.

6 Colour the butter cream grass green and put into a piping bag fitted with a small star nozzle (tip). Pipe strands of butter cream part of the way up the sides of the cake from the base upwards to represent grass. Arrange the pandas on top of the cake and by the side.

STEP 2

STEP 3

STEP 5

STEP 6

NOAH'S ARK

Most small children love animals and this is a good way to incorporate them into a birthday cake.

7-egg Victoria Sandwich (Sponge Layer
   Cake) mixture, any flavour (see page 8)
2 quantities butter cream (see page 15)
6 tbsp apricot jam, sieved (strained)
750 g/1½ lb/6 cups sugarpaste (see page
   16)
yellow, orange, red and blue liquid or paste
   food colourings
1 pkt long matchstick chocolates
plastic toy animal pairs

1 Grease and line 3 cake tins (pans) 28 × 18 × 4 cm/11 × 7 × 1½ inches. Divide the cake mixture evenly between the tins (pans) Bake in a preheated oven at 160°C/325°F/Gas Mark 3 for about 35–40 minutes until well risen and firm. Invert on wire racks and leave to set for 12–24 hours.

2 Sandwich 2 cakes together with butter cream, then round one end of the cake and cut the corners off the other end to shape it into a point from about 7.5 cm/3 inches back. Place on a cake board. Reserve the cut-off corners.

3 Cut the third cake into 2 pieces about 11 cm/4½ inches wide and sandwich together with butter cream. Place on top of the first cake to form the cabin. Use the cut-off corners to form a

roof and attach. Brush the whole ark with jam.

4 Colour 500 g/1 lb/4 cups of the sugarpaste brown. Roll out and use to cover the bows of the ark. Tint about a third of the butter cream yellow and spread over the deck of the ark.

5 Colour the remaining sugarpaste bright orange. Roll out and use to cover the sides of the ark cabin. Spread butter cream over the roof of the cabin.

6 Cover the roof of the cabin with chocolate matchsticks. Place matchsticks all round the edge of the deck, and make a gangplank with 3 or 4 chocolate matchsticks. Cut circles in the brown sugarpaste and attach for windows and a door. Make portholes out of orange sugarpaste.

7 Colour the remaining butter cream blue and put into a piping bag fitted with a star nozzle (tip). Pipe stars over the cake board to represent water. Place the pairs of animals on the deck of the ark, on the gangplank and about to board the ark.

HICKORY DICKORY DOCK CAKE

This cake is suitable for any child up to twelve years old. The hands of the clock can point to the age of the child, and the colourings can be varied to suit their preference.

STEP 3

STEP 4

STEP 5

STEP 6

3-egg and 4-egg Quick Mix Cake mixture (see page 8)
10 tbsp apricot jam, sieved (strained)
1 kg/2 lb/8 cups sugarpaste (see page 16)
blue, green and black liquid or paste food colourings
250 g/8 oz/2 cups royal icing (see page 15)

1 Grease and line a 23 cm/9 inch square cake tin (pan) and a 23 cm/ 9 inch deep round cake tin (pan). Spread the 3-egg cake mixture in the square tin (pan) and the 4-egg mixture in the round tin (pan). Bake in a preheated oven at 160°C/325°F/Gas Mark 3, about 1¼–1½ hours for the round cake and 50–60 minutes for the square. Invert on wire racks and leave for 12–24 hours.

2 Halve the square cake and sandwich together with 4 tablespoons of the jam. Place on a cake board and cut out a deep dip so the round cake fits into it. Trim the round cake evenly. Brush both cakes with the jam.

3 Colour half the sugarpaste pale blue. Roll it and use part to cover the cake on the board, moulding evenly. Cover the other cake's sides with almost all the remaining blue sugarpaste and push it into the dip in the first cake.

4 Colour a third of the remaining sugarpaste dark blue and half green. Roll out some of the green sugarpaste and use to cover the face of the clock, just overlapping the edge; then crimp it attractively. Roll the blue and the rest of the green sugarpaste into long sausage shapes. Twist together and place around the base of the clock face.

5 Use a scrap of the pale blue sugarpaste to form clock hands and attach to the face. Use the remaining pieces of sugarpaste to shape into mice with 2 ears, a long tail and a black nose, and mark the eyes with a cocktail stick (toothpick) (see page 78). Leave to dry.

6 Using royal icing and a piping bag fitted with a star nozzle (tip), pipe a border of stars around the base of the bottom end of the clock. Pipe small stars on the sides of the clock face and base, and a twisted circle on the face about 2.5 cm/1 inch in from the edge. With a No. 2 writing nozzle (tip), pipe the numbers on the clock and write 'Happy Birthday' and the child's name on the base of the cake. Pipe any extra decorations you might like on the clock. Leave to set, then attach the mice on and around the clock. Leave to set.

CHAPTER FIVE

Christmas Party Cakes

❀

Many children's parties are held around Christmas time. Some of them may be held to celebrate a birthday but most are probably seasonal parties arranged by schools, playgroups and clubs. A Christmas party is often rather different from an individual birthday party, for although there is no special 'guest of honour', a cake will add a focal point to the table, and provide something special to eat or to take home from the party. A special child's Christmas cake can also be a useful and enjoyable alternative to the usual fruit cake, which many children don't like.

The cakes illustrated here are only a few of the many possible ideas you might have for decorating a Christmas cake. Using the Sleigh, Snowman, Christmas Cracker and Stocking as inspiration, you could easily invent your own design and draw a template for other cakes such as a Christmas tree, Father Christmas, a nativity scene or a child in bed with a Christmas stocking, to name just a few, using all types of icings (frostings) and decorations.

For the child with a Christmas birthday, these cakes can be given a true birthday feel by adding candles and writing appropriate messages and the child's name in icing (frosting) – and remember too, the cake itself can be baked in a variety of flavours to suit all tastes, whatever the design.

Opposite: Not all cakes need to be decorated according to a formal scheme – sometimes it's more fun to pile on everything you can find, as in this mixture of dolls, sweets (candies) and numerous moulded and piped decorations.

STEP 3

STEP 4

STEP 4

STEP 5

CHRISTMAS CRACKER

This is an attractive cake that will look good at a birthday party alongside real crackers.

3-egg Madeira (Pound) Cake mixture (see page 10)

4 tbsp apricot jam, sieved (strained)

875 g/1³/₄ lb/7 cups sugarpaste (see page 16)

green, red, yellow and brown liquid or paste food colourings

1.5 metres/1¹/₂ yards red and silver ribbon, about 1–2.5 cm/¹/₂–1 inch wide

1 quantity butter cream (see page 15)

TO DECORATE:
teddy bears (see page 79)
parcels (see page 78)
holly leaves and berries (see page 78)
ivy leaves (see page 78)

1 Grease 2 special cylindrical loaf cake tins (pans) about 18 cm/ 7 inches long, 7 cm/3 inches in diameter and with a capacity of about 900 ml/ 1¹/₂ pints/3¹/₂ cups.

2 Divide the cake mixture evenly between the tins (pans), filling each two-thirds full. Place the tins (pans) on a baking sheet, keeping upright, and bake in a preheated oven at 160°C/325°F/Gas Mark 3 for about 50–60 minutes until firm. Cool for 10 minutes before inverting on a wire rack.

3 Cut one cake in half and trim diagonally around one edge of each half, and around each end of the long cake.

4 Using 175 g/6 oz/1¹/₂ cups of the white sugarpaste, roll out and cut discs to fit one end of the two short cakes. Roll a strip about 4 cm/1¹/₂ inches wide and place to overlap the ends by about 2.5 cm/1 inch, attaching with jam. Snip the edges with scissors. Attach one piece to each end of the long cake with butter cream and insert a plastic skewer through the centre to hold in place.

5 Colour the remaining sugarpaste bright green. Roll out so it is large enough to enclose the cake completely, overlapping by about 2.5 cm/1 inch at each end. Brush with jam, place the cake on it and wrap around, sealing edges, and pressing into the dips. Place on a cake board with the seam underneath. Snip the edges with scissors.

6 Tie the ribbons around the cracker, as in the photograph, and arrange holly leaves and berries, ivy, teddy bears and parcels on the cracker for decoration, attaching with butter cream. Leave to set.

STEP 2

STEP 3

STEP 4

STEP 6

SANTA'S SLEIGH

*A pretty cake with piles of Christmas parcels ready for Santa to deliver
to the children.*

5-egg Victoria Sandwich (Sponge Layer
    Cake) or Madeira (Pound) Cake mixture,
    any flavour (see page 8 or 10)
6 tbsp apricot jam, sieved (strained)
875 g/1³/₄ lb/7 cups sugarpaste (see page
    16)
red, brown, green, yellow and blue liquid or
    paste food colourings
1 quantity butter cream (see page 15)
few coloured sweets (candies)
2 long chocolate matchsticks
parcels (see page 78)
teddy bears (see page 79)
chocolate money and candy stick or rings
    (optional)

1 Grease and line a 23 cm/9 inch
square cake tin (pan). Spread the
cake mixture evenly in it. Bake in a
preheated oven at 160°C/325°F/Gas
Mark 3 for about 1–1¼ hours (1¼–1½
hours for Madeira (Pound) Cake) until
well risen and firm. Turn out and leave
on a wire rack for 12–24 hours to set.

2 Trim the cake and cut a 13 cm/
6 inch slice off one side. Cut the
slice to the same width as the sleigh, then
cut in half diagonally and place one piece
on each end, as in the photograph. Place
the cake on a board. Trim the remaining
piece to make a sack.

3 Brush the cake all over with jam.
Colour about 500 g/1 lb/4 cups of
the sugarpaste red. Roll out and use to
cover the cake. Colour 175 g/6 oz/1½
cups of the sugarpaste brown; use 90 g/
3 oz/¾ cup to make 2 rolls about 28 cm/
11 inches long and place along the base
of each side of the sleigh for runners. Tilt
each end up slightly and put paper towels
underneath to hold them in place.

4 Colour the butter cream deep
cream and place in a piping bag
fitted with a star nozzle (tip). Pipe
decorations around the sides of the
sleigh. Use the sweets (candies) to
decorate the sides of the sleigh and attach
a long chocolate matchstick on each side
with butter cream for the shafts.

5 Roll out the remaining brown
sugarpaste and use to cover the
other piece of cake for a sack, and place
in the sleigh. Colour the remaining
sugarpaste blue, yellow and green. Form
the green and blue into small parcels,
and mould the yellow into teddy bears.

6 Arrange the parcels, chocolate
money, teddy bears and candy stick
or rings in the sleigh, and attach with
butter cream.

STEP 2

STEP 3

STEP 5

STEP 6

MR SNOWMAN

Suitable for either a birthday or Christmas party, this snowman will please any child.

6-egg Victoria Sandwich (Sponge Layer Cake), Quick Mix Cake or Madeira (Pound) Cake mixture, any flavour (see page 8 or 10)
6 tbsp apricot jam, sieved (strained)
1.25 kg/2½ lb/10 cups sugarpaste (see page 16)
black, orange, yellow and green liquid or paste food colourings
250 g/8 oz/2 cups royal icing (see page 15) or 1 quantity butter cream (see page 15)
desiccated (shredded) or flaked coconut

1 Grease and line a roasting tin (pan) about 30 × 25 cm/12 × 10 inches. Spread the cake mixture evenly in it. Bake in a preheated oven at 160°C/325°F/Gas Mark 3 for about 50–60 minutes (1–1¼ hours for Quick Mix and Madeira (Pound) Cake), or until firm to the touch. Invert on a wire rack and leave to set for 12–24 hours.

2 Draw a template of a snowman, cut out and place on the cake. Cut around the template carefully and then cut out the arms and a hat from the cake trimmings. Place the body on a cake board and brush all over with jam. Brush the hat and arms with jam too.

3 Roll out about 750 g/1½ lb/6 cups of the white sugarpaste and use to cover the body and head.

4 Use the trimmings and another 125 g/4 oz/1 cup of the white sugarpaste to cover the arms of the snowman. Dampen the arms and attach them to the body.

5 Colour 45 g/1½ oz/⅓ cup of the sugarpaste black and use to make 3–4 round buttons, 2 eyes and a smiling mouth; dampen and attach. Colour 30 g/1 oz/¼ cup of the sugarpaste orange, shape into a carrot, dampen and attach for a nose.

6 Colour the remaining sugarpaste bright yellow and use to cover the hat and make a brim for it, and also to make a scarf. Attach to the snowman. Colour the royal icing or butter cream green and use to decorate the hat and scarf, using a small star nozzle (tip). Leave to set.

7 Sprinkle the coconut around the snowman to represent snow.

STEP 2

STEP 4

STEP 5

STEP 6

CHRISTMAS STOCKING

*Another appealing cake ideal for a Christmas party, or even the family
Christmas cake for a change.*

6-egg quantity Victoria Sandwich (Sponge
Layer Cake), Quick Mix Cake or Madeira
(Pound) Cake mixture, any flavour (see
page 8 or 10)
6 tbsp apricot jam, sieved (strained)
750 g/1½ lb/6 cups sugarpaste (see page
16)
red, green, yellow and blue liquid or paste
food colourings
holly leaves and berries (see page 78)
500 g/1 lb/4 cups royal icing (see page 15)
narrow Christmas ribbons
chocolate money

1 Grease and line a 30 × 25 cm/12 ×
10 inch roasting tin (pan). Spread
the cake mixture evenly in it. Bake in a
preheated oven at 160°C/325°F/Gas
Mark 3 for 50–60 minutes (1–1¼ hours
for Quick Mix and Madeira (Pound)
Cake) until well risen and firm to the
touch. Invert on a wire rack and leave to
set for 12–24 hours.

2 Draw a stocking shape on a sheet
of card the same size as the cake
and draw 3 or 4 shapes to use for parcels.
Cut out, place on the cake and cut
around the templates. Place the stocking
on a cake board and brush all over with
jam. Brush all over the pieces of cake for
the parcels too.

3 Colour three-quarters of the
sugarpaste red. Roll out and use to
cover the stocking. Trim off around the
base. Also make about 6 holly berries.

4 Colour 90 g/3 oz/¾ cup of the
sugarpaste green. Roll it out and
cut out 18 holly leaves. Use the rest to
cover one of the parcels.

5 Colour half the remaining
sugarpaste blue and the rest
yellow. Roll out the yellow sugarpaste
and cut 2 strips 2 cm/¾ inch wide and
some small stars. Place the strips across
the stocking. Use the remainder to cover
another of the parcels. Do the same with
the blue sugarpaste. Place the stars and
holly leaves in position.

6 Put some of the royal icing into a
piping bag fitted with a star nozzle
(tip) and the rest into a bag with a
writing nozzle (tip). Use the star nozzle
(tip) to pipe a decorative cuff around the
top of the stocking. Use the writing nozzle
(tip) to write 'Happy Christmas'. Attach
the holly leaves and berries in bunches.
Tie ribbons around the parcels and
position at the top of the stocking
together with the chocolate money.
Leave to set.

RECIPES & TECHNIQUES

CHOOSING AND LINING CAKE TINS (PANS)

Cake tins (pans) should be of good quality firm metal that conducts the heat evenly and will not dent during storage. Non-stick cake tins (pans) are available (when you should follow the manufacturer's instructions), otherwise tins (pans) must be greased with oil, butter or margarine and floured; or, most often, greased, lined either with greaseproof paper and greased again or lined with non-stick baking parchment.

To line a shallow rectangular tin (pan)

1. Cut a piece of greaseproof paper or non-stick baking parchment about 10 cm/ 4 inches larger than the tin (pan), or larger if deeper than 4 cm/1¹/₂ inches.

2. Stand the tin (pan) on the paper and make a cut from the corner of the paper to each corner of the tin (pan).

3. Grease the inside of the tin (pan), then put in the paper so it fits neatly, overlapping at the corners to give sharp angles. If using greaseproof paper, grease the paper once it is in place.

To line a loaf tin (pan)

Line the tin (pan) as described above, but cut the paper at least 15 cm/6 inches larger than the tin (pan).

Decorating cakes is an art which is increasing in popularity, and this book will provide you with a wide range of novelty cakes to suit boys and girls of all ages. The designs range from simple butter cream cakes to more ambitious sculptured designs. None of the designs is very difficult, but they do require a little concentration and a few hours to complete. On your first attempt, try one of the simpler designs, but with a little practice and patience you will soon be able to attempt any of these cakes, or even design your own.

VARIATIONS OF FLAVOUR

For Victoria Sandwich (Sponge Layer Cake) and Quick Mix Cake:

Orange or lemon flavour: omit vanilla flavouring (extract) and add 1 teaspoon finely grated orange or lemon rind for each egg used in the mixture.

Chocolate: add 2 tablespoons sifted cocoa powder for the 3-egg mix; 2¹/₂ tablespoons for the 4-egg mix, and so on, adding a further ¹/₂ tablespoon for each additional egg used in the mixture.

Coffee: add 1 tablespoon instant coffee powder for the 3-egg mix; 1¹/₂ tablespoons for the 4-egg mix; and so on, adding a further ¹/₂ tablespoon for each additional egg used in the mixture.

For Madeira (Pound) Cakes:

For both the following flavours, omit the lemon rind and juice.

Coffee: replace lemon juice with coffee essence.

Chocolate: replace the lemon juice with water and add 1 tablespoon sifted cocoa powder for the 2-egg mix; 1¹/₂ tablespoons for the 3-egg mix; and so on, adding a further ¹/₂ tablespoon for each additional egg used in the mixture.

MAKING AND USING PIPING BAGS

Use good-quality baking parchment or greaseproof paper for these.

1. Cut a piece of baking parchment to a square about 25–30 cm/10–12 inches. Fold in half to form a triangle.

2. Fold the triangle in half again to make a smaller triangle and crease firmly.

3. Open out and fold the bottom half of the triangle up to the central fold line.

4. Fold the bag over, and then over again, creasing each fold firmly. You should now have a cone shape. Secure the join with adhesive tape.

5. Cut off just the tip to allow the piping nozzle (tip) to fit into the bag so about one-third of the nozzle (tip) is showing. Fill the bag not more than half full with icing (frosting). Fold over the top of the bag to keep the icing (frosting) in place, then push the icing (frosting) down, so it is right in the nozzle (tip). It is now ready for use.

BASIC MIXTURE QUANTITIES FOR VICTORIA SANDWICH (SPONGE LAYER CAKE), QUICK MIX CAKE AND MADEIRA (POUND) CAKE

QUICK MIX CAKE

eggs	3	4	6
soft margarine	175g/6oz/^{3}/$_4$ cup	250g/8oz/1 cup	350g/12oz/1^1/$_2$ cups
caster sugar	175g/6oz/^{3}/$_4$ cup	250g/8oz/1 cup	350g/12oz/1^1/$_2$ cups
self-raising flour	175g/6oz/1^1/$_2$ cups	250g/8oz/2 cups	350g/12oz/3 cups
baking powder	1^1/$_2$ tsp	2 tsp	3 tsp
vanilla flavouring	^{1}/$_2$ tsp	^{1}/$_2$ tsp	^{1}/$_2$–^{3}/$_4$ tsp

VICTORIA SANDWICH (SPONGE LAYER CAKE)

eggs	2	3	4
butter or margarine	125g/4oz/^{1}/$_2$ cup	175g/6oz/^{3}/$_4$ cup	250g/8oz/1 cup
caster sugar	125g/4oz/^{1}/$_2$ cup	175g/6oz/^{3}/$_4$ cup	250g/8oz/1 cup
self-raising flour	125g/4oz/1 cup	175g/6oz/1^1/$_2$ cups	250g/8oz/2 cups
cold water	2–3 tsp	1 tbsp	1^1/$_2$ tbsp
vanilla flavouring	few drops	few drops	few drops

VICTORIA SANDWICH (SPONGE LAYER CAKE)

eggs	5	6	7
butter or margarine	300g/10oz/1^1/$_4$ cups	350g/12oz/1^1/$_2$ cups	425g/14oz/1^3/$_4$ cups
caster sugar	300g/10oz/1^1/$_4$ cups	350g/12oz/1^1/$_2$ cups	425g/14oz/1^3/$_4$ cups
self-raising flour	300g/10oz/2^1/$_2$ cups	350g/12oz/3 cups	425g/14oz/3^1/$_2$ cups
cold water	2 tbsp	2 tbsp	2^1/$_2$ tbsp
vanilla flavouring	^{1}/$_2$ tsp	^{3}/$_4$ tsp	^{3}/$_4$–1 tsp

MADEIRA (POUND) CAKE

eggs	2	3	4
butter or margarine	125g/4oz/^{1}/$_2$ cup	175g/6oz/^{3}/$_4$ cup	250g/8oz/1 cup
caster sugar	125g/4oz/^{1}/$_2$ cup	175g/6oz/^{3}/$_4$ cup	250g/8oz/1 cup
self-raising flour	125g /4oz/1 cup	175g/6oz/1^1/$_2$ cups	250g/8oz/2 cups
plain flour	60g/2oz/^{1}/$_2$ cup	90 g/3oz/^{3}/$_4$ cup	125g/4oz/1 cup
grated lemon rind	^{1}/$_2$–1 lemon	1 lemon	1^1/$_2$–2 lemons
lemon juice	2 tsp	1 tbsp	1^1/$_2$ tbsp

MADEIRA (POUND) CAKE

eggs	5	6	7
butter or margarine	300g/10oz/1^1/$_4$ cups	350g/12oz/1^1/$_2$ cups	425g/14oz/1^3/$_4$ cups
caster sugar	300g/10oz/1^1/$_4$ cups	350g/12oz/1^1/$_2$ cups	425g/14oz/1^3/$_4$ cups
self-raising flour	300g/10oz/2^1/$_2$ cups	350g/12oz/3 cups	425g/14oz/3^1/$_2$ cups
plain flour	150g/5oz/1^1/$_4$ cups	175g/6oz/1^1/$_2$ cups	200g/7oz/1^3/$_4$ cups
grated lemon rind	2 large lemons	2 large lemons	2–2^1/$_2$ lemons
lemon juice	2 tbsp	2 tbsp	2^1/$_2$ tbsp

To line a deep round or square tin (pan)

1. For a round tin (pan), cut one or two strips of greaseproof paper or non-stick baking parchment long enough to reach round the outside of the tin with enough to overlap, and wide enough to come 2.5 cm/1 inch above the rim of the tin. Fold the bottom edge up about 2 cm/^{3}/$_4$ inch and crease it firmly. Open out and make slanting cuts into the folded strip at 2 cm/^{3}/$_4$ inch intervals.

2. Place the tin (pan) on the paper and draw round the base then cut it out a fraction inside the line.

3. Grease the inside of the tin (pan), place the strip around the inside of the tin (pan) with the cut edge spread out over the base, grease, then place the circle in the base and grease overall.

4. For a square tin (pan), follow the instructions for a round tin (pan) but make folds into the corners of the long strips for the sides.

CHOOSING CAKE BOARDS
These should always be at least 5 cm/2 inches larger than the cake to allow for the decoration. Cakes over 25 cm/ 10 inches are best put on to thick cake drums, as the thinner cake boards do not offer sufficient support. For

larger cakes needing other than thick round or square boards, it is best to use two of the thinner boards stuck together, to prevent the cakes cracking as they are moved.

TEMPLATES
A template is a guide which is either placed on top of the cake and cut around to leave a shape, e.g. a teddy bear, clown or stocking; or it is placed on a royal or sugarpaste iced cake for the final decoration. It should be drawn on card or very stiff paper and then cut out. If the cake is very greasy, cut out the same shape in non-stick baking parchment to place under the template so it is not marked with grease. Use a very sharp and preferably serrated-edge knife to cut out cake shapes.

LIST OF EQUIPMENT
As with all cookery, the right equipment makes all the difference to the results. This list covers all the basic equipment necessary for making the cakes in this book. Some items can, of course, be improvised; but as you become more practised and more interested in cake decoration, you will gradually decide what you need and expand your collection of equipment as you find it necessary.

- selection of mixing bowls and basins, large and small
- measuring jugs

MOULDED DECORATIONS
Here are the methods for making the animals, flowers and other decorations featured in the recipes in this book. They can all be made from homemade or ready-made sugarpaste or marzipan.

Bells and shells for Open Book
(see page 54)
Bells can be shaped out of scraps of coloured sugarpaste by rolling them into balls in the palms of the hands and then pressing a hole in the base with a rounded plastic skewer. Leave to dry.

Make shells by placing coloured royal icing in a piping bag fitted with a large star nozzle (tip) and piping single shells on to non-stick baking parchment. Leave to dry.

Christmas parcels
(see pages 68 and 70)
Cut various shapes out of coloured sugarpaste or marzipan in squares and rectangles approx 2.5–5 cm/1–2 inches, and then leave to dry. Take very narrow ribbons in contrasting colours and tie them around the parcels so they look realistic.

Holly leaves and ivy leaves
(see pages 68 and 74)
Special cutters in various sizes can be bought to cut out these leaves. Colour the sugarpaste or marzipan a suitable green and roll out thinly on non-stick baking parchment. Either stamp out the shapes, remove from cutters, mark in veins with a knife and lay over a lightly greased rolling pin or spoon handles, so they dry in realistic curves. Or cut

sugarpaste into strips about 2 cm/³/₄ inch wide and 2.5–4 cm/1–1¹/₂ inches long, and using the sharp rounded end of a piping nozzle (tip) take 'cuts' out of each side of the strips to give holly leaves. Ivy leaves have 5 rounded points.

Make holly berries by rolling tiny scraps of red sugarpaste or marzipan in the palms of your hands into balls.

Mice for Hickory Dickory Dock cake
(see page 64)
These can be made in any colour you like but the ears should be lined with white or pale pink sugarpaste and a scrap of black sugarpaste is needed for the noses.

Use 30–90 g/1–3 oz/¹/₄–³/₄ cup sugarpaste for the mouse body, removing a scrap for the ears, and piece for the tail; shape into a teardrop shape with a point for the nose. Mark in 2 eyes with a cocktail stick and make 2 slits above the eyes for ears.

Shape the ear scraps of sugarpaste into 2 very thin circles, then attach 2 smaller circles of white or pink sugarpaste. Pinch together at the base and inset in the slits, tipping the ears forward slightly.

Roll out the tail piece into a very thin sausage, make a tiny hole at the rear of the mouse and insert the tail. Add a scrap of black sugarpaste for the nose and then add 3 or 4 short lengths of flower stamens (available from specialist cake decorating shops) for the whiskers and leave to set.

Pandas for Panda's Picnic cake
(see page 60)
These need 45–90 g/1¹/₂–3 oz/¹/₄–³/₄ cup sugarpaste for each panda and of each

78

amount two-thirds should be white and
the remainder coloured black.

For each panda, shape just over two-
thirds of the white sugarpaste into a ball
for the body and the rest into a smaller
ball for the head. Remove a tiny piece of
black sugarpaste to make the eyes, ears
and a nose.

Halve the remaining black sugarpaste
and roll each piece into a sausage about
7–10 cm/3–4 inches long, depending on
the size of the panda. Bend one piece into
a U shape for feet and legs and place the
body on top.

Insert half a wooden cocktail stick
(toothpick) through the body and impale
the head on top.

Attach the arms around the body as in
the photograph, then add tiny pieces for
ears in slits in the top of the head; and
add 2 eye patches and a nose. Using a
cocktail stick (toothpick), mark eyes in
the centre of the black eye patches and
mark 4 claws on the feet and arms. Leave
to set.

Sugarpaste flowers
(see page 57)
Colour sugarpaste or marzipan as
required and then roll out on non-stick
baking parchment. Using a multi-petal
flower cutter, stamp out the flowers. If
you like, you can press a sugared mimosa
ball in the centre of each flower, pressing
up the sides of the flowers slightly. Leave
to dry.

For the piped flowers in the grass,
simply fill a piping bag fitted with a star
nozzle (tip) with butter cream or royal
icing and pipe large stars. Again, place a
mimosa ball in the centre, if you like.

Teddy bears
(see pages 68 and 70)
These can be made in any colour you like
using 45–90 g/1^1/$_2$–3 oz/^{1}/$_3$–^{3}/$_4$ cup
sugarpaste or marzipan for each bear.
They are made in a similar way to the
pandas, but all in one colour, and the
piece for the head is shaped with a point
for the nose and the ears are pinched out
at the top of the head. Mark the eyes with
a cocktail stick (toothpick) and add a
scrap of black for the nose.

Tiny teddy bears
(see pages 68 and 70)
For each bear use 30–45 g/1–1^1/$_2$ oz/
^{1}/$_4$–^{1}/$_3$ cup sugarpaste or marzipan
coloured yellow, gold or pale brown, and
a tiny scrap of deeper brown for the nose.
From one piece of sugarpaste shape a
bear's head and body, then shape a
pointed nose and pinched up ears, and
then arms and legs from the body. Mark
the eyes and 4 claws on each foot and
arm with a cocktail stick (toothpick).
Finally add a scrap of darker sugarpaste
for the nose and leave to dry.

USING SWEETS (CANDIES) FOR DECORATIONS
Round and coloured chocolate or candy
sweets are ideal for adding eyes, noses,
buttons, etc. to novelty cakes. The
colours can be varied to suit the colour
scheme and there are various sizes
available too. Chocolate matchsticks are
also useful for fences, tree trunks,
railings, etc. Silver, gold and coloured
dragées of various sizes are also good.
Strips of liquorice and candy can be used;
the red strips make good mouths.

- spatulas
- spoon measures
- tablespoons and teaspoons
- wooden spoons
- weighing scales
- large and small palette knives (spatulas)
- pastry brushes
- short skewers and wooden cocktail sticks (toothpicks)
- ruler
- icing(frosting) comb or scraper
- small plastic containers with airtight lids
- greaseproof paper and non-stick baking parchment
- selection of basic icing (frosting) nozzles (tips), including fine, medium and thick writing nozzles (tips) and small, medium and large star nozzles (tips)
- large piping bags
- paper piping bags (buy or make)
- compass
- tweezers
- sets of cocktail and aspic cutters
- large and small scissors
- electric hand mixer
- nylon or good metal sieve
- small flat or balloon whisk
- selection of liquid and/or paste food colouring
- icing (frosting) turntable
- food colouring pens
- rolling pin and small icing (frosting) rolling pin
- sets of plain and fluted biscuit cutters

INDEX